A WINNING CREW
THE 1936 U.S. OLYMPIC ROWING TEAM

BY BETSY RATHBURN
ILLUSTRATION BY EUGENE SMITH
COLOR BY GERARDO SANDOVAL

Black Sheep

BELLWETHER MEDIA • MINNEAPOLIS, MN

STRAY FROM REGULAR READS WITH BLACK SHEEP BOOKS. FEEL A RUSH WITH EVERY READ!

This edition first published in 2024 by Bellwether Media, Inc.

No part of this publication may be reproduced in whole or in part without written permission of the publisher.
For information regarding permission, write to Bellwether Media, Inc., Attention: Permissions Department,
6012 Blue Circle Drive, Minnetonka, MN 55343.

Library of Congress Cataloging-in-Publication Data

Names: Rathburn, Betsy, author. | Smith, Eugene (Illustrator), illustrator.
Title: A winning crew : the 1936 U.S. Olympic rowing team / by Betsy Rathburn ; [illustrated by Eugene Smith].
Description: Minneapolis, MN : Bellwether Media, Inc., 2024. | Series: Black sheep : Greatest moments in sports |
    Includes bibliographical references and index. | Audience: Ages 7-13 years | Audience: Grades 4-6 | Summary:
    "Exciting illustrations follow the 1936 U.S. Rowing Team as they compete in the Olympics. The combination of brightly
    colored panels and leveled text is intended for students in grades 3 through 8"– Provided by publisher.
Identifiers: LCCN 2023017823 (print) | LCCN 2023017824 (ebook) | ISBN 9798886875119 (library binding) |
    ISBN 9798886875614 (paperback) | ISBN 9798886876994 (ebook)
Subjects: LCSH: University of Washington–Rowing–History–Juvenile literature. | Olympic Games (11th : 1936 :
    Berlin, Germany)–Juvenile literature. | Rowing–United States–History–Juvenile literature. | Rowers–United States–Biography-
    Juvenile literature. | Olympic athletes–United States–Biography–Juvenile literature.
Classification: LCC GV796 .R3 2024 (print) | LCC GV796 (ebook) | DDC 797.12/309730904-dc23/eng/20230523
LC record available at https://lccn.loc.gov/2023017823
LC ebook record available at https://lccn.loc.gov/2023017824

Editor: Christina Leaf   Designer: Andrea Schneider

Printed in the United States of America, North Mankato, MN.

TABLE OF CONTENTS

THE OLYMPIC DREAM...................4

ON THE ROAD.........................8

GOING FOR THE GOLD..................14

MORE ABOUT THE 1936.................22
    U.S. OLYMPIC ROWING TEAM

GLOSSARY............................23

TO LEARN MORE.......................24

INDEX...............................24

Red text identifies historical quotes.

THE OLYMPIC DREAM

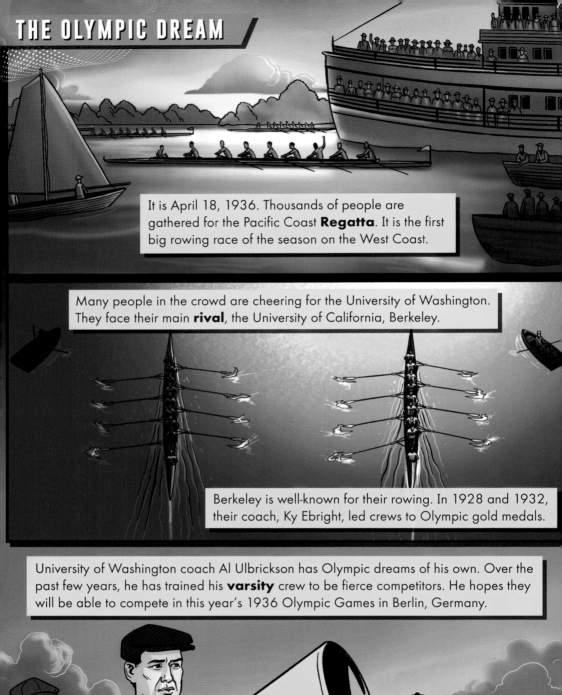

It is April 18, 1936. Thousands of people are gathered for the Pacific Coast **Regatta**. It is the first big rowing race of the season on the West Coast.

Many people in the crowd are cheering for the University of Washington. They face their main **rival**, the University of California, Berkeley.

Berkeley is well-known for their rowing. In 1928 and 1932, their coach, Ky Ebright, led crews to Olympic gold medals.

University of Washington coach Al Ulbrickson has Olympic dreams of his own. Over the past few years, he has trained his **varsity** crew to be fierce competitors. He hopes they will be able to compete in this year's 1936 Olympic Games in Berlin, Germany.

But the team must win several races before they can **qualify**.

The Pacific Coast Regatta starts out well for the Berkeley crew. They quickly pull ahead. For a while, Washington works hard to match their **stroke rate**.

But then Washington **coxswain** Bobby Moch decides to slow his crew's pace.

The slower pace lets the crew row more powerfully. Much of the crew grew up on farms or have worked in logging, which has made them extremely strong.

They pull their oars through the water again and again.

Moch's direction pays off. The Washington **shell** pulls ahead, beating Berkeley by three boat lengths. They even set a new course record!

The first-place finish is only the beginning of Washington's rowing season. For the rest of the spring, the crew trains hard. For practice, they often race Washington's junior varsity (JV) crew.

Okay, crews. The junior varsity boat gets a head start.

Even when their opponents have a head start...

Give me ten big ones!

...the varsity team easily pulls ahead. They have learned to row as one, listening to their coxswain for guidance. This gives them the ability to win even the toughest races.

As he watches his crew get better and better, Coach Ulbrickson begins to believe that they have a real chance at the Olympics.

Maybe they will go all the way to Berlin.

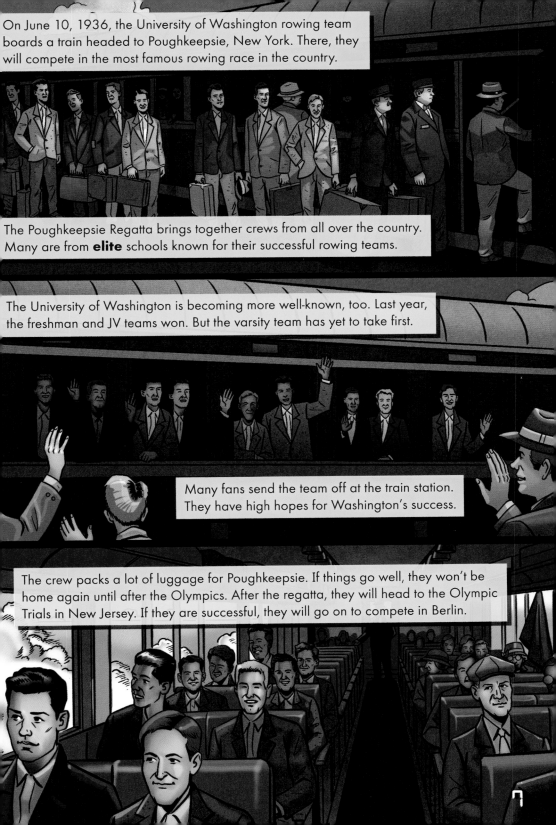

On June 10, 1936, the University of Washington rowing team boards a train headed to Poughkeepsie, New York. There, they will compete in the most famous rowing race in the country.

The Poughkeepsie Regatta brings together crews from all over the country. Many are from **elite** schools known for their successful rowing teams.

The University of Washington is becoming more well-known, too. Last year, the freshman and JV teams won. But the varsity team has yet to take first.

Many fans send the team off at the train station. They have high hopes for Washington's success.

The crew packs a lot of luggage for Poughkeepsie. If things go well, they won't be home again until after the Olympics. After the regatta, they will head to the Olympic Trials in New Jersey. If they are successful, they will go on to compete in Berlin.

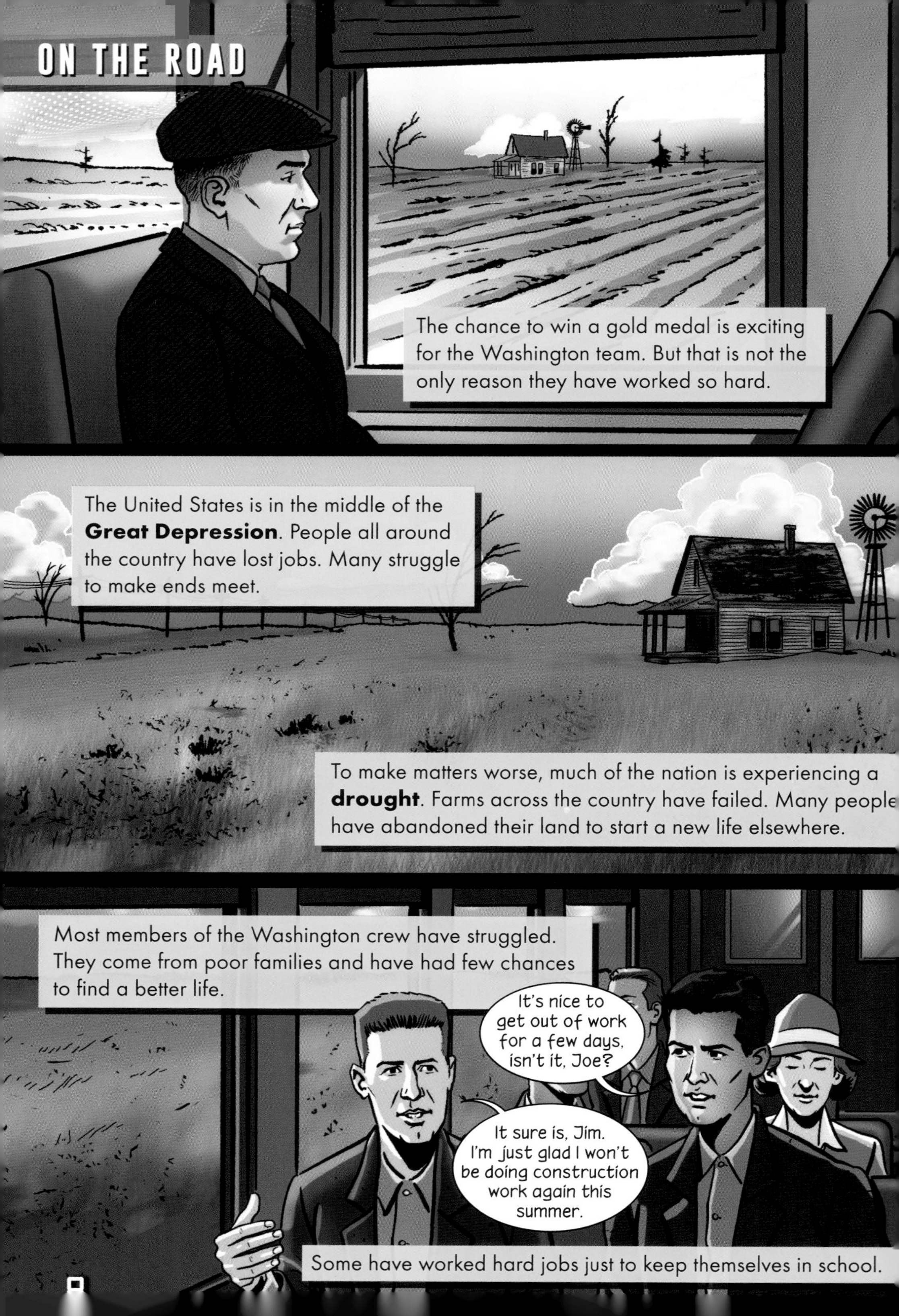
ON THE ROAD
The chance to win a gold medal is exciting for the Washington team. But that is not the only reason they have worked so hard.
The United States is in the middle of the Great Depression. People all around the country have lost jobs. Many struggle to make ends meet.
To make matters worse, much of the nation is experiencing a drought. Farms across the country have failed. Many people have abandoned their land to start a new life elsewhere.
Most members of the Washington crew have struggled. They come from poor families and have had few chances to find a better life.
It's nice to get out of work for a few days, isn't it, Joe?
It sure is, Jim. I'm just glad I won't be doing construction work again this summer.
Some have worked hard jobs just to keep themselves in school.

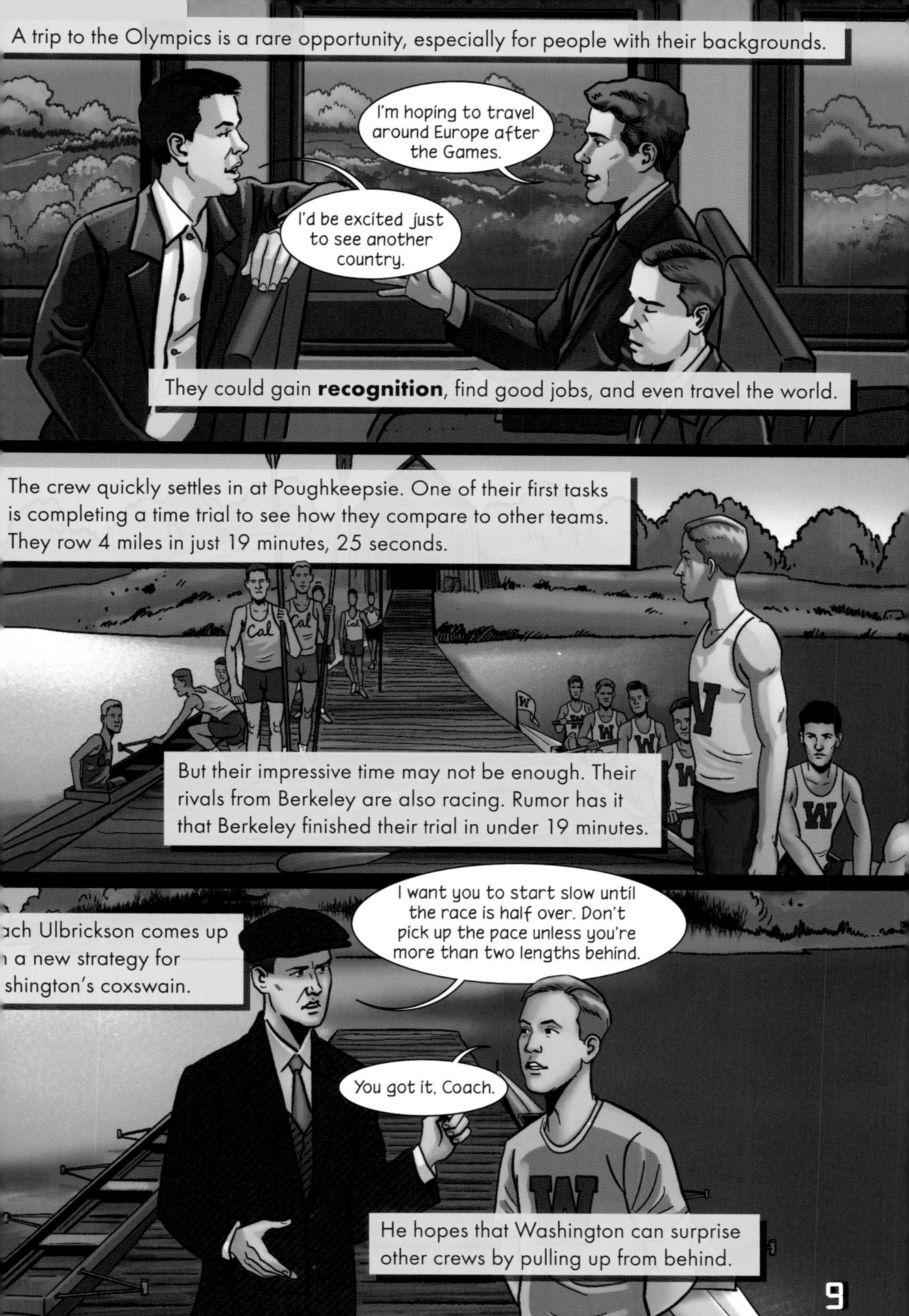
A trip to the Olympics is a rare opportunity, especially for people with their backgrounds.
I'm hoping to travel around Europe after the Games.
I'd be excited just to see another country.
They could gain **recognition**, find good jobs, and even travel the world.
The crew quickly settles in at Poughkeepsie. One of their first tasks is completing a time trial to see how they compare to other teams. They row 4 miles in just 19 minutes, 25 seconds.
But their impressive time may not be enough. Their rivals from Berkeley are also racing. Rumor has it that Berkeley finished their trial in under 19 minutes.
ach Ulbrickson comes up a new strategy for shington's coxswain.
I want you to start slow until the race is half over. Don't pick up the pace unless you're more than two lengths behind.
You got it, Coach.
He hopes that Washington can surprise other crews by pulling up from behind.

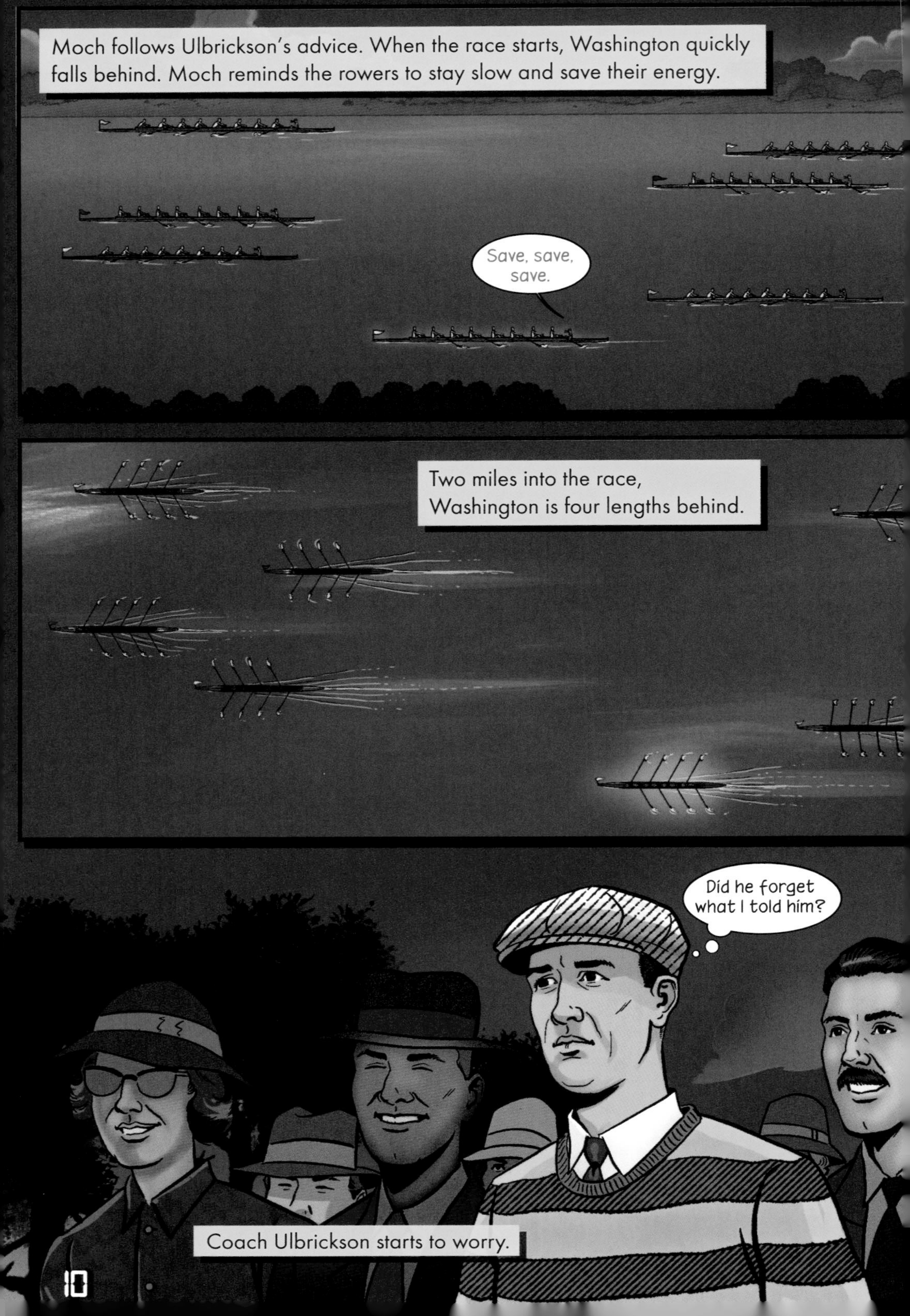
Moch follows Ulbrickson's advice. When the race starts, Washington quickly falls behind. Moch reminds the rowers to stay slow and save their energy.
Save, save, save.
Two miles into the race, Washington is four lengths behind.
Did he forget what I told him?
Coach Ulbrickson starts to worry.

But Ulbrickson doesn't know that Moch has his own plan.

Take your time. We can catch those boys any time we want.

Okay! Now! Now! Now!

In the last half-mile, Moch tells the crew to increase their stroke rate.

Coming from behind, the Washington crew pulls past the other **exhausted** teams. The crowd roars as Washington crosses the finish line.

In the Washington shell, the crew is thrilled. Not only have they beaten their Berkeley rivals for a second time, but their victory makes a trip to the Olympics seem possible.

The Olympic Trials are held about two weeks after the Poughkeepsie Regatta win. The crew travels to Princeton, New Jersey. Here, they have two races. Their **preliminary** race pits them against two other **contenders**.

Washington easily wins, earning a trip to the final qualifying race.

The final race is a bigger challenge. Washington again faces Berkeley, along with the New York Athletic Club and Pennsylvania.

Slow and steady now.

Washington gets off to a poor start. When the race begins, they are instantly in last place. But they aren't worried.

Washington is in third place about three-quarters into the race. But then...

Here's California! Here's where we take California!

...they increase their stroke rate and pull ahead of Berkeley.

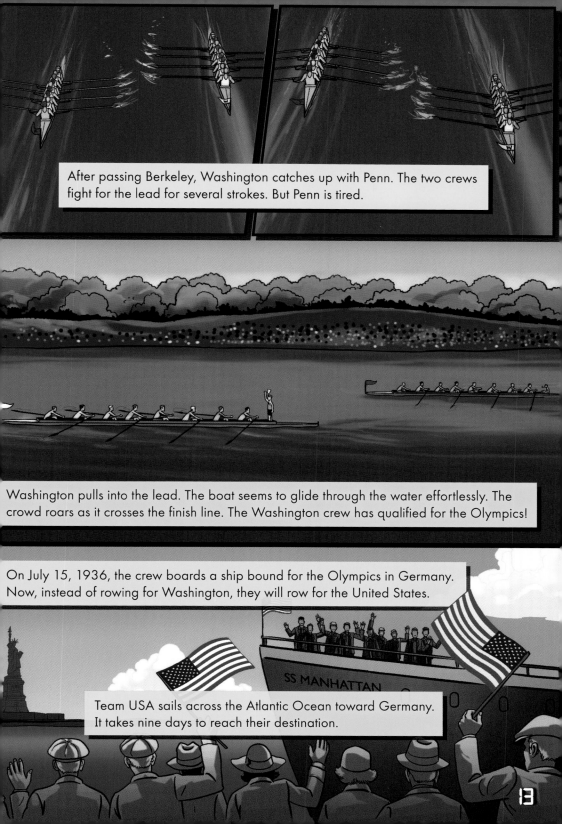

After passing Berkeley, Washington catches up with Penn. The two crews fight for the lead for several strokes. But Penn is tired.

Washington pulls into the lead. The boat seems to glide through the water effortlessly. The crowd roars as it crosses the finish line. The Washington crew has qualified for the Olympics!

On July 15, 1936, the crew boards a ship bound for the Olympics in Germany. Now, instead of rowing for Washington, they will row for the United States.

Team USA sails across the Atlantic Ocean toward Germany. It takes nine days to reach their destination.

The German people busy themselves getting ready for the Olympics. They want to prove that they are better than other nations. They paint, clean the streets, and wash windows. But this cheery look holds darker truths.

In the past several years, the Nazi Party has come to power in Germany. Its leader, Adolf Hitler, has made many changes.

»Burn them all!«

He has banned many books that do not agree with his views. He has also arrested people who do not agree with him.

Hitler's worst **restrictions** are on Germany's Jewish people. They are not allowed to vote, work certain jobs, or visit certain places. They are not considered German citizens.

Before the Olympics, Hitler hides any proof of their mistreatment. He plans to use the Games to make Germany look good. That way, no one will try to stop him from carrying out his plans to **eliminate** Jewish people.

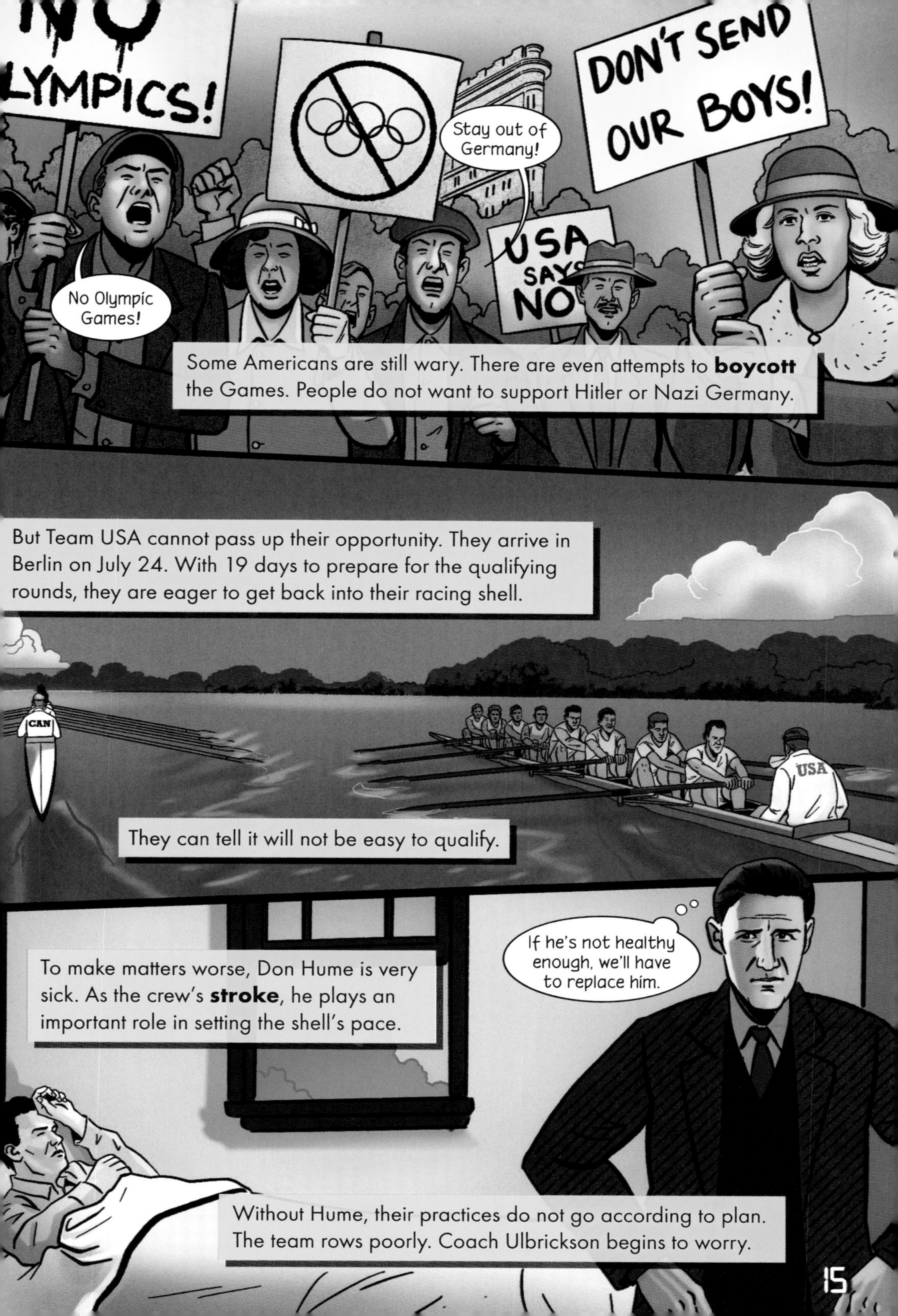

LYMPICS!
DON'T SEND OUR BOYS!
Stay out of Germany!
USA SAYS NO
No Olympic Games!
Some Americans are still wary. There are even attempts to **boycott** the Games. People do not want to support Hitler or Nazi Germany.
But Team USA cannot pass up their opportunity. They arrive in Berlin on July 24. With 19 days to prepare for the qualifying rounds, they are eager to get back into their racing shell.
CAN
USA
They can tell it will not be easy to qualify.
To make matters worse, Don Hume is very sick. As the crew's **stroke**, he plays an important role in setting the shell's pace.
If he's not healthy enough, we'll have to replace him.
Without Hume, their practices do not go according to plan. The team rows poorly. Coach Ulbrickson begins to worry.

With their chances of an Olympic gold on the line, the team begins to tighten their focus. They concentrate on rowing, tuning out any news from home or Germany.

Nice and easy, okay? We've got this.

By August 12, the day of the preliminary race, they feel good about their chances again. Hume is well enough to join the crew in the shell. The team's confidence soars with their stroke back in the boat.

In this race, Team USA faces 4 of the 13 other rowing crews. If they win, they advance to the finals. If they lose, they must compete in another race to qualify.

Unfortunately, Team USA gets off to a poor start. They quickly fall to last place.

But it doesn't last long. Soon, crews start getting tired. They begin to fall behind. Team USA takes its chance.

Now, boys! Now! Give me ten!

Nearing the finish line, the crew comes neck and neck with the British. Team USA increases its stroke rate and glides past the British and over the finish line.

»And Team USA moves on to the final round!«

But the crew doesn't have time to celebrate the win. After Team USA crosses the finish line, Don Hume collapses in the shell.

Don! Are you okay?!

Though they have qualified for the finals, the team is unsure whether Hume will be able to move forward with them.

On the morning of the final race, Hume is too sick to get out of bed. Coach Ulbrickson begins to make plans.

We're going to have to use our **alternate**.

I understand.

But the rest of the crew disagrees with the coach's decision.

We talked it over, Coach. We can't race without him.

If you put him in the boat, Coach, we will pull him across the line.

USA

If you really feel that way, then we had better bring him along.

17

Outside, the water is rough and choppy. But that doesn't stop Germany from dominating the day's other rowing competitions.

Again and again, German boats take the win. They come in second place in only one race. The crowd's excitement for the final race grows.

While rain falls, the teams take their places at the starting line. Though Team USA earned a place in the best lane with the calmest water, German officials assign it to Germany instead.

Team USA is given the worst lane with the choppiest water.

The crowd is loud, and the rough water is distracting. An announcer calls for the teams to get ready, but Team USA does not hear it. The starting flag drops...

...and the only teams left at the starting line are Great Britain and Team USA.

The crew immediately begins trying to make up for it. They row hard against the choppy water. At the 500-meter mark, they rise to fifth place...

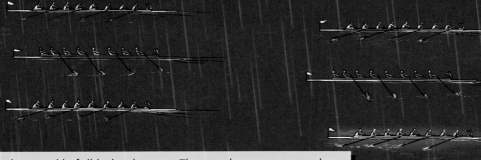

...but quickly fall behind again. The rough water means they have to work harder than usual to row at the same speed.

Moch knows the crew must make a move. He calls for Hume to increase the stroke rate. At first, Hume does not respond.

But he eventually snaps to attention. Team USA glides to third place. They join Italy and Germany in the battle for first.

As the boats near the finish line, the roar of the crowd becomes deafening. The Team USA crew can no longer hear Moch's directions.

DEUTSCHLAND!

Come on! Give me one more! We're almost there!

Moch pounds on the boat to tell the crew to row faster.

They do. Team USA begins rowing faster than they ever have before. As they reach the finish line, they are neck and neck with Germany and Italy.

All three teams reach the finish line at almost the same time.

ZIEL

Once they cross it, no one knows who won.

Then, finally...

»Team USA wins!«

Team USA crossed the finish line just before Italy and Germany. They have beaten Nazi Germany and won the Olympic gold.

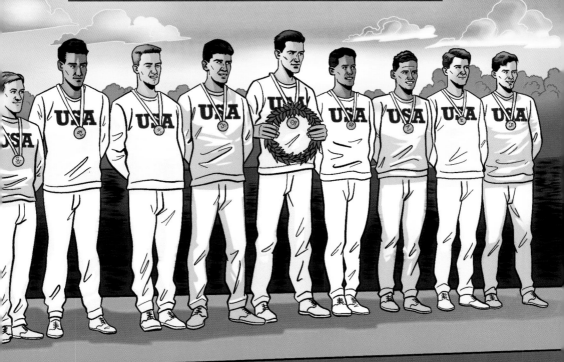

With practice and teamwork, the little-known team from Washington goes down in Olympic history!

MORE ABOUT THE 1936 U.S. OLYMPIC ROWING TEAM

- The Olympic medal race drew the biggest rowing race crowd in Olympic history at the time. Around 75,000 people were in the crowd.

- The team used racing shells hand-built by George Pocock. This famous British builder was later added to the Washington State Sports Hall of Fame.

- In 1948, Al Ulbrickson coached another team to Olympic gold. His four-man rowing crew won the gold medal at the Olympic Games in London.

- After the Olympics, Bobby Moch worked as assistant coach of the University of Washington rowing team under Al Ulbrickson. He later became head coach at MIT.

- A movie was made about the 1936 U.S. Olympic rowing team. It is called *The Boys in the Boat*.

1936 U.S. OLYMPIC ROWING TEAM TIMELINE

APRIL 18, 1936
The University of Washington crew wins the Pacific Coast Regatta

JULY 5, 1936
The crew races in the Olympic Trials, winning a spot in the Berlin Olympics

JUNE 22, 1936
The crew wins the Poughkeepsie Regatta

AUGUST 14, 1936
Team USA wins the Olympic gold

1936 OLYMPICS · · · · · · ·   **EUROPE**
BERLIN, GERMANY

GLOSSARY

alternate—a person who takes the place of another person who cannot make it

boycott—to refuse to do or support something

contenders—people or teams who are competing against others to win

coxswain—the person in charge of a crew boat; the coxswain steers the boat and gives directions but does not row.

drought—a time of little or no rain

eliminate—to get rid of something or someone entirely

elite—known for being better than others

exhausted—very tired

Great Depression—a time in world history when many countries experienced economic crisis; the Great Depression began in 1929 and lasted through the 1930s.

preliminary—related to something that happens before something else

qualify—to be allowed to participate in a certain event

recognition—acknowledgment of success

regatta—a competition made up of a series of boat races

restrictions—rules or laws that prevent people from doing certain things

rival—a long-standing opponent

shell—a lightweight boat used for crew racing

stroke—the member of a rowing crew who sets the rate of rowing for the other members

stroke rate—the speed at which a crew team rows

varsity—related to the main team that represents a school

TO LEARN MORE

AT THE LIBRARY

Bowman, Chris. *Wilma Rudolph and the 1960 Olympics*. Minneapolis, Minn.: Bellwether Media, 2024.

Brown, Daniel James, adapted for young readers by Gregory Mone. *The Boys in the Boat: the True Story of an American Team's Epic Journey to Win Gold at the 1936 Olympics*. New York, N.Y.: Viking, 2015.

Gitlin, Marty. *The Great Depression*. Ann Arbor, Mich.: Cherry Lake Publishing, 2022.

ON THE WEB

FACTSURFER

Factsurfer.com gives you a safe, fun way to find more information.

1. Go to www.factsurfer.com
2. Enter "1936 U.S. Olympic rowing team" into the search box and click 🔍.
3. Select your book cover to see a list of related content.

INDEX

Berlin, 4, 6, 7, 15
boycott, 15
Germany, 4, 13, 14, 15, 16, 18, 19, 20, 21
Great Depression, 8
historical quotes, 10, 11, 12, 16, 17, 19
Hitler, Adolf, 14, 15
Hume, Don, 15, 16, 17, 19
Moch, Bobby, 5, 6, 9, 10, 11, 12, 16, 17, 19, 20

Olympic Trials, 7, 12, 13
Pacific Coast Regatta, 4, 5
Poughkeepsie Regatta, 7, 9, 10, 11,
qualify, 4, 12, 13, 15, 16, 17
Ulbrickson, Al, 4, 6, 9, 10, 11, 15, 17
University of California, Berkeley, 4, 5, 9, 11, 12, 13
University of Washington, 4, 5, 6, 7, 8, 9, 10, 11, 12, 13, 21